CW00820262

Masonic Samaritan Fund
Medical Care and Support

The Sign of a
MASON

Lewis Masonic

Medical Care and Support

The Masonic Samaritan Fund

Registered Charity 1001298

The Masonic Samaritan Fund (MSF) is a grant-making charity that supports Freemasons and their dependants who have an identified medical need, are waiting for treatment and cannot afford private medical care. Since it was established in 1990, the fund has supported over 8,000 applicants of all ages who have faced a long wait for, or been unable to access, treatment via the NHS. Demand for support from the MSF continues to increase, as does the cost of meeting that demand. The proceeds from the sale of this book will be thankfully received and faithfully applied in support of those in need of medical care and support. If you would like to know more about the work of the MSF and the support available, please contact the fund direct on 020 7404 1550 or by email: mail@msfund.org.uk.

The Sign of a
MASON

Lewis Masonic

MARTIN FAULKS

First published 2008

ISBN 978 085318 289 4

Published by Lewis Masonic

an imprint of Ian Allan Publishing Ltd,
Hersham, Surrey KT12 4RG.
Printed in England by Ian Allan Printing Ltd,
Hersham, Surrey KT12 4RG.

Visit the Lewis Masonic website at
www.lewismasonic.com

The First Lodge meeting under the auspices of the newly appointed Worshipful Master was off to a good start, and the Secretary was reading the minutes of the last meeting – the installation ceremony. At one stage he paused, and said to the W.M., "There were 27 Past Masters and 43 members in attendance. Will you take their names as read Worshipful Master?"

"No," said the W.M. "If you wouldn't mind, I would like to hear their names."

The disgruntled Secretary duly obliged and paused to say, "I received 17 apologies Worshipful Master; will you take their names as read?"

"I would much rather hear their names, Worshipful Brother Secretary," said the W.M. The Secretary read out the names, but the tone of his voice did little to disguise his feelings. The ceremony that evening was the second degree, and the Secretary was delivering the explanation of the tracing board. When he reached the part 'and there fell on that day forty and two thousand Ephramites,' he turned to the W.M. and said, "Will you take their names as read, Worshipful Master?"

●

Q: How many Masons does it take to change a light bulb?
A: Change it? Never! My grandfather donated that bulb to the Lodge!

●

A Brother had committed murder, and on arrival at the gallows he remonstrated with the hangman, declaring, "You cannot go through with this execution! I'm a Mason!"

The hangman replied, "I don't know anything about that. Step off with your left foot."

●

The Sign of a Mason

A Newly installed W.M was determined to pack as much as possible into his year of office, and to that end he visited Brother George, who had recently taken up residence in a nursing home. During the drive to the nursing home, the W.M. revelled in the thought that George would be very impressed to have a visit from his W.M. Ten minutes into his visit, the W.M. began to doubt if George had recognised him so he asked, "George, do you know who I am?"

"No," said George. "But if you ask the matron, she will tell you who you are."

●

A nervous Brother was performing the first degree charge. As his nerves got the better of him, his actions became faster and faster. To make matters worse, as he fidgeted in his chair, he knocked his gavel off the pedestal. One wise Past Master remarked to another, "Did you hear the Masonic boom?"

•

The ceremony had reached the point when every officer had been appointed with the exception of the Tyler. The director of ceremonies took up his position in front of the newly appointed W.M., stood to order and froze. The D.C. and the W.M. looked at each other without a word being spoken. Eventually, the silence was broken when a well-intentioned prompter shouted in a broad cockney accent, "Who's yah Tylah?" In reply, a Brother said "Montague Burton."

•

A senior member of a Lodge was well known for organising fraternal visits: between two and five visits per year. However, one such trip that made the others look very ordinary was the fraternal visit to one of the oldest Lodges in the USA. Such was the interest of the members of his Lodge, plus those from other Lodges, he was able to fill every seat on the plane.

With their visit over, they all gathered in the departure lounge waiting for their flight home. It was then the pilot sought out the Brother organiser with the news that the flight home would be unique as every member of the crew was a Mason. A buzz of excitement spread through the assembled Masons, which was heightened when someone suggested that the flight could be even more unique if they carried out a ceremony 40,000 feet above the Atlantic. Everyone thought the suggestion was an excellent one except the Lodge Secretary, who felt they should have higher authority, such as permission from the Provincial Grand Master.

The dauntless Brother organiser dashed to the nearest telephone to ring the P.G.M. forgetting that the time in the UK would be different to that in the States. In fact, it was 3.40am when the P.G.M. was called to the phone and, as he didn't get to bed until gone one o'clock, he wasn't best pleased. However, he listened attentively and said that it would be fine for them to hold a ceremony on board the plane, but politely pointed out that they could have done so without asking him. Before putting down the phone, he said to the Brother organiser, "When the officers are being appointed, it would be my pleasure to appoint you as Tyler."

•

"The festive board is going well," said one Brother to the J.W. "Shall we let them have fun a little more or would you like to do your toast for the visitors now?"

•

I am a Staffordshire Mason, but my commitment to Masonry was cemented when I realised the depths of support that Brothers provide to one another. One bad winter, I visited the Baldock Lodge of Harmony in Hertfordshire. The ceremony was enthralling and it was with great amazement that I left the Festive Board to discover five inches of snow had fallen whilst we were in the Lodge. I stood at the top of the steps and said to myself, "I don't fancy driving 110 miles in that."

"Then don't," said a voice at my elbow. It came from one of the visitors who lived nearby. He invited me into his home to sit by a roaring log fire, enjoy a welcome nightcap and a good night's sleep. I met his wife and in no time was deep in conversation about Masonry and its attributes. It was only when I got home the next morning that I realised I hadn't phoned my wife to explain where I was. She was furious and demanded to know who had so graciously put me up. I told her I didn't really know, except that it was one of the Masters from a Hertfordshire Lodge. I went to work in deep trouble, but when I got home I found that my enterprising wife had obtained a list of every Master of every Lodge in Hertfordshire.

"Did one of them confirm my story?" I asked.

"Oh yes," she said. "They all did."

•

The working tool of a Past Master: In an orchestra,
the triangle is a minor percussion instrument. It is used
infrequently and has little significance in the overall texture
of the music but adds brilliance and emphasis in the quieter
passages of a performance. But as we are not all musical
or melodic Masons, we must apply this tool to ourselves.
Masonically, it teaches us that having vacated the Chair
of King Solomon and contemplated the difficulties which
accompany that great responsibility, having boldly
perfected our Ritual and in spite of all distractions and
advice delivered, we are reminded, as Past Masters, to sit
quietly in the East and observe the proceedings of the
Lodge, to contribute little and chime in only at moments
of particular gravity with telling sage comments (or the
occasional 'wrong' prompt).

•

A man told his wife that he wasn't feeling too well. She
suggested that he should make an appointment to see his
doctor. The GP examined him but said he could not find

the cause of the problem. He was then advised to go and see a specialist at the local hospital. A specialist examined him and said he had some bad news. He was informed that he had a very rare disease called Yellow 41 and had only six months to live.

When he arrived home, he was totally devastated. After explaining the situation to his wife she pointed out that, as his days were numbered, if there was anything he wanted to do, this was the time to do it. He gave the matter some thought and eventually admitted that he had always wanted to play bingo but could never find the time.

"We will go tonight," said his wife. So that evening they made their way to the local bingo hall. Much to everyone's surprise, he won every game throughout the entire evening. At the end of the session he approached the M.C. to collect his winnings.

The M.C. said, "I have run this organisation for many years and I have never come across anyone who has won everything right through the whole evening. You are a very lucky man."

"Lucky man?" came the reply. "I've got Yellow 41."

"I don't believe it," said the M.C. "You have even won the raffle!"

•

Q: A Lodge of Masons wants to change a bulb and have only a small table to stand on. How long will it take to change the bulb?

A: They'll never do it. They'll be too busy helping each other get on the table!

•

If you have a problem remembering Ritual, spare a thought for this couple. While on a road trip, an elderly couple had lunch at a roadside restaurant. After finishing their meal, they left the restaurant to resume their trip. The elderly woman unknowingly left her glasses on the table and didn't miss them until they had been driving for twenty minutes and, to add to their aggravation, they had to travel quite a distance before they could find the opportunity to turn around and return to the restaurant.

On the return journey, the husband turned into the clichéd grouchy old man. He fussed, complained and scolded his wife relentlessly. The more he chided her, the more agitated he became- he wouldn't let up for one minute. To her relief, they finally arrived at the restaurant. As the woman got out of the car and hurried inside to retrieve her glasses, the old geezer yelled, "While you're in there, you might as well get my hat and the credit card!"

•

A man new to Masonry was talking with his friend and said, "We have Grand Officers in our Lodge who are very religious."

"How come?" said his friend.

"Well, every time our new master does the Ritual, they put their heads in their hands and say, 'Oh my God!'"

•

One of our Brethren was telling me that he has just returned from Australia where he visited an outback Lodge. At the Festive Board, he noticed pieces of meat hanging from the ceiling. Curiosity got the better of him and he asked the Brother sitting next to him what the decorations were doing there.

"Ah," said the Brother. "One of our Brothers, who has now passed on, left us a legacy that provided meat for our barbie with the proviso that the Brother requiring a free meal only had to jump up and pull meat off the string. However, if he failed to do so, he had to buy drinks all round."

"Oh," I said. "Did you have a go?"
"No," he replied. "The steaks were too high."

It has been reported in our Lodge that a motorcar was spotted travelling on the M25 at a very slow speed. A motorway patrol was alerted, found the car and pulled it over. On enquiry, a policeman found that an old Provincial Officer was driving his Provincial Master to a meeting. The policeman asked why the driver was proceeding so slowly, and he replied that it was the M25.

"Yes, it is. But why so slowly?" asked the policeman. After further questioning, it dawned on him that the driver was convinced that, as it was the M25, he was restricted to 25mph. At this point, groans and whimpers were heard coming from the back of the car. Shining a torch into the backseat, the policeman discovered the Provincial Master curled into a foetal position, with his head in his hands and a look of terror on his face.

"My God!" cried the copper. "What on earth is wrong with him?"

"I don't know," the Provincial Officer replied. "He's been like that since we turned off the B182."

This is especially for members of the Royal Ark Mariner Lodges. In the year 2008, the Lord came unto Noah, who was now living in England, and said, "Once again the Earth has become wicked and overpopulated, and I see the end of all flesh before me. Build another ark and save two of every living thing along with a few good humans."

He gave Noah the drawings saying, "You have six months to build the ark before I start the unending rain for forty days and forty nights." Six months later, the Lord looked down and saw Noah weeping in his yard but with no ark in sight. "Noah!" he roared. "I'm about to start the rain. Where is the ark?"

"Forgive me, Lord," begged Noah, "but things have changed. I needed building regulations approval and I've been arguing with the fire brigade about the need for a sprinkler system. My neighbours claim that I should have obtained planning permission for building the ark in my garden because it is a development of the site, even though in my view it is a temporary structure.

"We then had to appeal to the Secretary of State for a decision. The Department of Transport demanded a bond be posted for the future costs of moving power lines and overhead obstructions to clear the passage of the ark's move to the sea. I told them that the sea would be coming to us, but they would hear nothing of it. Getting the wood was another problem. All the decent trees have preservation orders on them and we live in a 'site of special scientific interest' set up in order to protect the Little Owl. I tried to convince the environmentalists that I needed the wood to save the owls, but again no-go. When I started gathering the animals the RSPCA sued me. They insisted that I was confining wild animals against their will. They argued the accommodation was too restrictive and it was cruel and inhumane to put so many animals in a confined space.

"Then the County Council, the Environment Agency and the Rivers Authority ruled that I couldn't build the ark until they'd conducted an environmental impact study on your proposed flood. I'm still trying to resolve a complaint with the Equal Opportunities Commission on how many disabled carpenters I'm supposed to hire for my building team. The trades unions say I can't use my sons. They insist I have to hire only accredited workers with ark-building experience. The health and safety people insist on having one of their inspectors on site twenty four hours a day at my expense. To make matters worse, Customs and Excise seized all my assets, claiming I'm trying to leave the country illegally with endangered species. So forgive me Lord, but it would take at least ten years for me to finish this ark."

Suddenly the skies cleared, the sun began to shine and a rainbow stretched across the sky. Noah looked up in wonder and asked, "You mean you're not going to destroy the world?"

"No," said the Lord. "The British Government beat me to it!"

●

The Sign of a Mason

Two men out driving passed a Masonic Lodge. One said to the other, "I have always wondered what that building was."

"I'm sure it's a betting shop," said his friend.

"I'm sure you're wrong," he replied.
"Anyway, what makes you think that?"

"Well, as I was walking past the other day, I saw two gentlemen talking and I overheard one of them saying, 'So far I have had a first, two seconds and one third.'"

•

A mason went to a friend's house to practise his Ritual and listened to his friend initiate his parrot. He was amazed that the parrot could repeat the whole first degree Ritual and asked as if the bird knew the second degree Ritual. "No," said his friend. "He is rubbish and falls off the perch when he does the signs."

An initiate was cycling to the Lodge for his initiation when the chain broke. Fortunately his friend came along in a car and he told him what had happened. His friend handed him a rope and explained that instead of pedalling, he would be towed. After the ceremony, his friend asked him how he felt. "I am amazed," he replied. "How did that man inside the door know how I got here on a free wheel and a cord?"

●

Q: How many Past Masters does it take to change a
     light bulb?
A: None. That's the Secretary's job.

●

A doctor was examining one of his patients who was very nervous. The doctor realised that he was a fellow Mason and, to put him at his ease when the examination was over, he said: "You may now retire in order to restore yourself to your own personal comforts."

To which the patient replied, "Yes, and on my return you will no doubt render the usual charge!"

•

In the days of yore, when hanging was the penalty for murder, a condemned man was taken to the scaffold and asked if he had anything to say before his execution took place. He said, "I blame it all on Freemasonry."
"Why is that?" the hangman asked.

"The man I murdered was a Freemason. The policeman who arrested me was a Freemason. The prosecutor was a Freemason. The judge was a Freemason."

The hangman replied, "Is that all you have to say?"

The condemned man nodded.

"Then with the left foot take one pace forward."

The Sign of a Mason

A man is drifting in a hot air balloon when the clouds
become dense and navigation becomes impossible.
He lets air escape from the balloon and descends through
the clouds where he can see a man riding a bicycle.
The balloonist calls down, "Where am I?"

The cyclist looks up and shouts, "You are in a balloon."
"You must be the local Lodge I.P.M.," replied the balloonist.

"Why, yes I am! But how on earth did you know that?"
replied the startled cyclist.

"Well, your information is one hundred per cent accurate
and one hundred per cent useless!"

●

Three men are debating who has the greatest claim to the
oldest professional: a surgeon, a solicitor and the W.M.
The surgeon said that as God created woman from the rib
of man, it was obviously the work of a surgeon.

"Nonsense!" replied the solicitor. "It says in the Bible that God created order out of chaos, which was obviously the work of a legal mind such as mine."

"Sorry, gentlemen," the W.M. concluded. "We are the oldest. After all, who do you think created the chaos in the first place?"

●

The Pope and the W.M. are debating who has the greatest powers. So the challenge is laid down – whoever can walk on water will be judged the greatest. The Pope starts first and is soon up to his neck in water and gives in. The W.M. walks across the lake with only the soles of his shoes touching the water.

"I have to concede," the Pope said.

As they walk away, the S.W. says to the W.M., "Should we tell him where the stepping stones are?"

•

Our W.M. claims to be a good golfer but when he tried to drown himself, he failed because he couldn't keep his head down long enough.

•

The mediacal definition of 'brain death' is the man who enjoys the J.W.'s jokes about the visitors!

•

If wind surfers do it standing up and rugby players do it with odd shaped balls, Freemasons do it craftily.

•

Three past masters were discussing what epitaphs they wanted carved on their tombstones when they died. The first said, "I want it to state that I served my Lodge well,

put our finances in order and resolved all problems.
It should also mention that it was I who implemented
many of our social programmes."

The second said, "I want them to say that I raised more
new Brothers then any Past Master we ever had. I raised
the standard of our Ritual in the Lodge. They should say
that I instituted community programmes and brought
true Masonic ideals to our non-Masonic neighbours."
They both looked to the third Past Master and asked
him what words he would like on his tombstone.

He said, "Look, he's moving!"

●

LODGE HUMOUR: The Structure of the Lodge

The Right Worshipful Master,
Leaps tall buildings in a single bound,
Is more powerful than an express train,

Is faster than a speeding bullet,
Walks on water and gives policy to God.

The Worshipful Senior Warden,
Leaps short buildings with a single bound,
Is more powerful than a goods train,
Is just as fast as a speeding bullet,
Walks on the water if the sea is calm and talks with God.

The Worshipful Junior Warden,
Leaps short buildings with a running start and a
favourable wind,
Is almost as powerful as a goods train,
Is faster than a speeding air gun pellet,
Walks on water of a paddling pool and talks with God
if special dispensation is given.

The Senior Deacon,
Barely clears a garden hut,
Loses a tug-of-war with a train,
Can fire a speeding bullet,

Swims well and is occasionally addressed by God.

The Junior Deacon,
Makes splat marks on the wall when trying to leap buildings,
Is run over by trains,
Can sometimes handle a gun without inflicting self-injury,
Doggie paddles and talks with the animals.

The Inner Guard,
Runs headlong into buildings,
Recognises trains two out of three times,
Is not issued ammunition,
Can stay afloat with a life jacket and talks to walls.

The Steward,
Falls over doorsteps when trying to enter buildings,
Says, 'Look at the choo choos',
Wets himself with a water pistol,
Plays in mud puddles and mumbles to himself.

The Secretary,
Lifts buildings and walks under them,
Kicks trains off the tracks,
Catches speeding bullets in his mouth and eats them,
Freezes water with a single glance,
He is God!

●

Visiting our Lodge in the rural backwater of Aberdeen, a Brother from London was talking to the Secretary about the well-known and important men that belonged to his fine London Lodge. "So, have any big men been born around here?" he asked the Secretary.

"No, the best we can do are babies. Different in London I suppose?"

●

The R.W.M. was in hospital recovering from an operation and the Secretary visited to update him on the meeting he had missed. "Your apologies were duly noted and I informed the Brethren assembled the reason you were unable to attend. The W.S.W. proposed and the W.J.W. seconded that you be wished a speedy recovery. The proposal was duly put to the Brethren and the result was 22 for, 18 against and 7 abstentions."

●

The M.W.G.M.M. was planning a Grand Lodge trip to visit the Grand Lodge of Hawaii. He asked the Grand Secretary to investigate the protocols and made a special request that he find out the local pronunciation of Hawaii. Was it 'Ha-wai-ee' or 'Ha-vai-ee'? The Grand Secretary duly called his counterpart in Hawaii and, after discussing the nature of the planned visit, asked the question. "Ha-vai-ee," replied the voice on the phone.

"Great! Thanks for your help," the Grand Secretary replied.

"You're velcome."

•

A mason was telling one of his fellows about the trouble he was having with his Ritual. His friend said he knew a Brother who sold parrots that know the Ritual and prompt you when you have any trouble. So the next day he went to the shop. After strict examination, the owner pulled a curtain to reveal three parrots. The first was wearing a R.W.M.'s apron, the second a DoC's apron and the third a P.M.'s apron.

"How much is the one with the R.W.M.'s apron?"

"£6,000. He knows all the Ritual, including the inner workings and will always prompt you when you get stuck," the owner said.

"No, too expensive. What about the one with the DoC's apron?"

"Well, that one is only £2,000. He doesn't know the inner

workings, but knows most of the Ritual and will always prompt you when learning," replied the owner.

"No, still too much I'm afraid. What about the one wearing the P.M.'s apron?"

"Oh, I can let you have him for just £10!" the owner suggested.

"Why so cheap? He must know all the Ritual and the inner workings."

"Oh yes," said the owner. "He knows all the Ritual, but when you make a mistake all he does is mutter 'Tut, tut, tut'!"

•

After recieving his apprentice degree, a candidate returned home. His wife asked him what happened. Recalling that he couldn't give up the secrets of his degree, all he could muster was, "Well honey, there were a lot of walkers, talkers and holy men." With a somewhat confused expression, she asked what he meant.

He explained, "Well, I couldn't see anybody in the room and was guided by the walkers. I would stop and then somebody would talk. I was then guided around some more, was stopped and then somebody else talked."

His wife then asked, "That explains the walkers and talkers. What about the holy men?"

He pondered for a moment and replied, "Well, often when somebody finished talking, they would hold their heads in their hands and say, 'Oh my God!'"

●

A ninety-five year old Past Master got married to a lovely bride of eighteen. As they climbed into bed on their wedding night, he asked, "Did your mother teach you the facts of life?" His new wife blushed and shyly shook her head. "That's a pity. I've forgotten what they are."

●

A new E.A. was chatting to some of his Brethren in the Harmony after the meeting. "I think I've got most of the signs, but what's the meaning of the one where you put your finger in your ear and whistle?"
His proposer replied, "It means that the Past Masters' hearing aids are turned up too high again!"

●

Old past masters never die. However, you'll have to become one before you find out why.

●

A candidate was sitting with his proposer and seconder at Harmony after his initiation. "Who was that sitting on the

W.M.'s left?" he asked.

"That was the I.P.M.," his proposer replied.

"And on his right?" asked the candidate.

"That was the Provincial Grand Master."

"I see," said the candidate. "So why did the W.M. keep interrupting them while they were doing the degree?"

•

ONE DAY, OUR Brother discovers a small village somewhere in the north east of Scotland. He is curious to know if there is a Masonic Lodge, so he takes a walk through the village and after some time he finds a path called 'Mason's Road'. Thinking that the path might lead to the Masonic Temple, he follows it. At the end of the pathway he sees a building, which appears somewhat rotten and out of use for quite a while. Our Brother tries to open the door and, surprisingly, it's not locked. He goes inside and finds dust and spider webs everywhere. In front of a particular door sits a skeleton wearing an apron and collar, holding a sword in its bony hand.

"Oh my goodness!" says our Brother in surprise as he enters the Lodge room. In puzzlement, he sees skeletons adorned in collars and aprons throughout the room: the R.W.M., Wardens, Organist and Deacons – all skeletons. He looks around the room and studies the seats of the Secretary and Treasurer. Under the hand of the Treasurer, he finds a small piece of paper, a note possibly intended to have been passed to the Secretary. So our Brother picks up the note, blows away the dust and reads 'If nobody prompts the W.M. soon, we'll be sitting here forever!'

●

The W.M. and his two Wardens went golfing one day. As they were about to tee off the first hole, the course marshal asked if a young woman could join them.

Being a charitable group they all agreed. She turned out to be a scratch golfer, but on the eighteenth hole she drove the green in two and was about to putt for an eagle. She then told the three Brothers that if any one of them helped her make the putt she would be eternally grateful. The Junior Warden looked at the putt and told her it was uphill and broke to the right. The Senior Warden, being a more expert workman, looked at it and said, "That is partially correct but five inches from the hole, it breaks to the left."

●

The W.M. then took his turn. He looked at the putt and the young lady very carefully, then went over to the ball, picked it up and exclaimed, "It's a gimme!"

●

Q: How many Past Masters does it take to change a light bulb?

A: One. However, it will take him a year to find an

authentic antique Edison bulb in keeping with the ancient landmarks.

●

At three in the morning, a policeman comes across a tipsy Mason walking unsteadily down a street. "Where are you going at this time of night?" asks the policeman.

"I'mmm g-g-going to a lecture o-o-on Fffreeemassonnry!" slurs our hero.

"Where can you get a lecture on Freemasonry at this hour?" queries the policeman.

"F-from mmy wife w-when I get home!"

●

I do not attend the meetings for I've not the time to spare. But every time they have a feast you will surely find me there.

I cannot help with the degrees for I do not know the work.
But I can applaud the speakers and handle a knife and fork.
I'm so rusty in the Ritual, it seems like Greek to me.
But practice has made me perfect in the Knife and Fork
Degree.

•

A travelling saleman is standing at a bar in a small village
and starts to berate and criticise the Craft. He then asks
the barman if he wants to hear a funny joke about the
Masons. The barman reveals that he is a Mason, the other
barman is a Mason, the people beside him are Masons, and
the man entering the bar is also a Mason. "So do you still
want to tell your joke?" asks the barman.

"Not if I have to explain it five times over!" the salesman
replied.

•

A doctor is about to carry out a physical on a Jewish patient. "I won't let anyone touch me who doesn't have kosher hands!" says the patient. Seeing the depth of his conviction, the doctor calls round the hospital to find a Jewish doctor to perform the examination. Finally, he finds one on the eighth floor, explains the predicament and asks if the Jewish doctor could assist.

"Sorry, I've got my own problems here," says his colleague. "I've got five Catholics who won't pee in a Mason jar."

•

A brother was driving home after a Lodge meeting and Harmony. Sure enough, a blue light followed the car and he pulled over to the side of the road. Thinking that the policeman might be a Freemason, he placed his driving licence and insurance papers within his Ritual book. When the policeman asked for his documents he made a great play of taking it from his Ritual book, but the policeman gave no reaction whatsoever. Our Brother was then asked to blow into the breathalyzer, which proved positive. He gave the sign of distress, but was ignored. The policeman started to write notes in his pocket book. At this point, the Brother was desperate to relieve himself, so he asked the police officer if he could retire to the bushes in order to restore himself to his personal comforts.

"Certainly sir, and on your return you will give your attention to a charge."

●

A newly raised M.M. was going for a job interview and knew that his interviewer was a prominent member of the Craft. He took great care to wear his ring, lapel-badge, cufflinks, neck chain and other Masonic jewellery. The interview was going well, although he had not been given any indication of recognition. At the end of the interview, he was asked as to what salary package he was looking for and said, "Oh, £55,000 a year and six weeks' paid holiday."

The interviewer looked him straight in the eye and replied, "We'll halve it and you begin!"

●

In the days of the Old West, a young fellow held up a bank, and in so doing shot and killed the teller. Several people witnessed his terrible crime and were able to identify him as he rode out of town. A posse was formed and the fugitive was captured and sent to jail back in the town. He was duly tried and sentenced to hang for his crime. On the appointed day of the execution, a scaffold was erected outside the jail. As the fellow was led up the stairs to the scaffold, the judge read his sentence and asked him if he had anything to say.

"I sure do, judge. If it wasn't for the Masons, I wouldn't be here." The judge enquired as to what he was referring. "Well, the sheriff who pursued me is a Mason, as was most of the posse. The jury was mostly Masons, and you, judge, are a Mason. If it wasn't for the Masons, I wouldn't be here."

That being all he had to say, the judge ordered the hangman to proceed. The hangman placed a hood over the fellow's head, put the rope around his neck, took him by the left arm and said, "You will now take one short step with your left foot."

●

Did you hear about the Lodge that was holding meetings in the function room of a local hotel while its temple was undergoing renovations? One evening, a travelling salesman asked the receptionist who the men in the function room were. The receptionist replied, "Oh, those are the Masons."

The salesman said, "I've always wanted to join the Masons. Do you think that they would let me in?"

"Oh no," the receptionist answered. "They're very exclusive. Why, you see that poor bloke standing outside the door with a sword in his hand? He's been knocking for six months and they still won't let him in!"

●

The wife of a new Mason was constantly pestering her husband to tell her what happens at Lodge meetings. He finally gave in and said that they hire a stripper to dance naked. "Do you look?" she asked.

"Of course I look," he said, "Otherwise I'd be an Oddfellow."

●

Q: How many Past Masters does it take to change a light bulb?
A: Why change it...it always worked before?

●

Jock, an eager new office-bearer was out walking along the riverbank one day when a frog called out to him. "Hey there! I'm not a frog. If you kiss me, I'll turn into a beautiful woman." Without breaking his stride, Jock leant down, scooped up the frog and put it in his pocket. The frog piped up, louder. "If you kiss me and turn me back into a woman, I'll stay with you for a year." Jock kept walking. More desperate, the frog shouted, "Look, I'm really a princess. But I want to be a woman again. If you kiss me, I'll stay with you forever and do whatever you want." Jock still kept on walking. "Hey, look at me!" the frog screamed. Jock stopped, took the frog out of his pocket and looked it square in the eyes. "What's wrong with you? I'm a beautiful, rich princess willing to marry you, have your children and do whatever you want. Why won't you kiss me?" the frog demanded.

"I'm not long in office in my Lodge," said Jock. "A girlfriend would take up a lot of time and make it more difficult to learn the Ritual. A talking frog on the other hand will always get me a free drink at the bar!"

●

Some years back, just after the introduction of random breath testing, the police officers of a small country town had to show the community that the scheme against drink driving was having an effect. They decided to stake out the local Masonic Hall. As the night wore on, a Mason slowly came down the stairs, searched his pockets several times before finding his keys, and after having difficulties in locating the lock, eventually got in his car. The moment he started the engine, the two police officers approached and asked him to 'blow in the bag'. He did as he was told, and, to the amazement of the officers, the test proved negative.

Fearing that the bag was faulty, the officers tried again but with the same results. Sure of a conviction, they escorted him to the police station for a blood test. However, it was negative. Upset with their lack of damning evidence, the officers asked him what he had done that evening. "Well, the Master was there, the Secretary was there, the Treasurer was there. In fact, all the office-bearers were there and we all had a great time," he answered.

"So, what's your office?" one of the policeman asked.

"Can't you guess?" says our man. "I was the Senior Decoy!"

●

In days of old, a Brother Knight had his squire polish his best armour, and had his groom prepare his best charger. On seeing this activity his fair lady said "If you're going to that Lodge again, you'd better be back before 10.30pm or I'm raising the drawbridge and you're out for the night."

"Yes, dear," he replied as he packed his apron into his saddlebag and headed off to the meeting. At 10.13pm, there had been a bit of Harmony at the close of the meeting. With alarm, Sir Knight looked at his moondial and noticed the time. He downed the last of his mead, grabbed his apron, leapt to his charger and set off at full gallop towards the castle. 10.20pm and he was on the home straight. However, though the castle was in view the horse was tiring. In desperation, the knight spurred his steed for the final run as time ran out. 10.29pm and with only yards to go, the drawbridge started to rise. With a feat of unsurpassed horsemanship, he climbed to his feet and leapt from the saddle to the edge of the rising drawbridge. As his fingertips bit into the edge, the weight of the armour was too much to bear. Slowly releasing his grip on the wood, he looked down and said, "Oh well, so moat it be!"

●

A well-known Brother once wanted to affiliate to a Lodge only a few miles away from his Mother Lodge. He went through the motions of obtaining a demit from his Mother Lodge and presenting it to the Secretary of his chosen Lodge, along with his application for affiliation. When asked what his reasons for wanting to move were, he replied, "Health reasons."

"That's a fairly unusual reason for wanting to move. If I'm not being too nosy, what's the problem?" asked the Secretary.

"They got sick of me over there!"

●

"Goodness Katie be quiet!" scolded mummy. "Stop shouting like that. Be more like your little brother Tommy and play quietly."

"He's got to be quiet, Mummy. He's playing at being 'Daddy coming home from the Lodge'," said Katie.

"So why are you shouting?" asked mummy.

"Because I'm pretending to be you!"

●

A Businessman arrived home at eight in the morning. His wife, sitting at the breakfast table, angrily demanded where he'd been. "I was working late with Janice, the new temp, and when we finished we went out for something to eat. We had a few drinks, a bottle of wine, and then went on to a club for a bit of a laugh and a few more drinks. Well, we ended up back at her flat and one thing led to another…"

"Don't lie to me. You were at that bloody Lodge again, weren't you?"

•

Jock was the foreman of a building site. He was sitting in his trailer when two bricklayers walked in. "You'll have to do something about Jim," says one. "He's got a personal hygiene problem."

"He's a labourer lugging bricks around all day," said Jock. "Of course he's going to get a bit sweaty."

"Well, we're not working with him unless you do something about it!" the bricklayers replied before storming out.

So Jock calls Jim into the trailer and says, "There's no easy way to say this, so I'll just come straight to the point. B.O."

Jim appeared puzzled and replied, "A.Z."

"Get back to work, Jim," says Jock. "I've got to go and fire those two brickies."

●

Within a large town in America, there were three Masonic Lodges: Prince Hall, F & AM and AF & AM. All three had a serious problem with squirrel infestations in their buildings, Therefore, each Lodge, in its own fashion, had a special meeting to deal with the problem. The Prince Hall decided that the squirrels were predestined to be in the Lodge and that they would just have to live with them.

The F & AM decided they should deal with the squirrels in the movement's style of community responsibility and social action. They humanely trapped the animals and released them in a park on the edge of town, only to find that within three days, they had returned to the Lodge building.

The AF & AM Masonic Lodge had several lengthy special meetings, allowing all members to voice their opinions, and finally decided to have a secret ballot to vote the squirrels in as members of the Lodge. They now only see them during the P.M. night.

●

Q: What's the difference between a Mason's wife and a wheelie bin?
A: The wheelie bin gets out once a week.

●

Ten Master Masons, happy, doing fine.
One listened to a rumour, then there were nine.

Nine Master Masons, faithful, never late.
One didn't like the Master, then there were eight.

Eight Master Masons, on their way to heaven.
One joined too many clubs, then there were seven.

Seven Master Masons, life dealt some hard licks.
One grew discouraged, then there were six.

Six Master Masons, all very much alive.
One lost his interest, then there were five.

Five Master Masons, wishing there were more.
Got into a great dispute, then there were four.

Four Master Masons, busy as could be.
One didn't like the programmes, then there were three.

Three Master Masons, was one of them you?
One grew tired of all the work, then there were two.

Two Master Masons with so much to be done.
One said 'What's the use?', then there was one.

One Master Mason, found a Brother – (true!).
Brought him to the Lodge, then there were two.

The Sign of a Mason

Two Master Masons didn't find work a bore.
Each brought another, then there were four.

Four Master Masons saved their Lodge's fate.
By showing others kindness, then there were eight.

Eight Master Masons, loving their Lodge's bright sheen.
Talked so much about it, they soon counted sixteen.

Sixteen Master Masons, to their obligations true.
Were pleased when their number went to thirty-two.

If we can't put our troubles at the Lodge's door.
It's our own fault for harming the Lodge we adore.

Don't fuss about the programmes or the Master in the
East. Keep your obligation by serving even the very least.

●

APPOINTED STEWARD

Q: How were you first prepared to be made a Steward?

A: My coat sleeves and shirt sleeves were rolled up and a corkscrew thrust into my hand.

Q: What is a corkscrew?

A: An implement fashioned like a winding staircase which our ancient Brethren ascended to receive their beer.

Q: What is beer?

A: A peculiar product of alchemy, veiled in mystery, and illustrated by labels.

Q: How is it usually depicted in our assemblies?

A: By a couple of hops near to a barrel of water.

Q: Where did our ancient Brethren go to receive their beer?

A: To a convivial room adjacent to the Lodge.

Q: How did they receive it?

A: In tankards and half tankards.

Q: Why in this peculiar manner?

A: In half tankards, well knowing that the same could

easily be replenished and in tankards, from the great reliance that they placed on the mildness of the brew in those days.

Q: What were the names of the two embellishments which decorated the doorway or entrance to this convivial room?

A: That on the left was called "Bass," and that on the right "Guinness."

Q: What are their separate and conjoint significations?

A: The former denotes "strength", the latter "sustenance" and when conjoined in a haphazard manner "instability". But when consumed without untoward excess they assist in promoting the spirit of friendship and harmony which should at all times characterise assemblies of Freemasons.

•

Q: How many Masons does it take to change a light bulb?

A: Seven. One to do the work and six Past Masters on the sidelines to prompt him.

•

WHY MEN MAKE BETTER FRIENDS:

FRIENDSHIP BETWEEN WOMEN: A woman didn't
come home one night. The next morning she told her
husband that she had slept over at a friend's house.
The man called his wife's ten best friends. None of them
knew anything about it.

FRIENDSHIP BETWEEN MEN: A man didn't come
home one night. The next morning he told his wife that he
had slept over at a friend's house. The woman called her
husband's ten best friends, eight of whom confirmed that
he had slept over, and two said that he was still there.

•

THE SIGN OF A MASON:

A Mason was sitting with a number of non-Masons down at his local pub, where the landlord was also a Brother. Numerous jokes were cracked at the expense of the Fraternity, and the Mason was called upon to show them a Mason's sign. One of the men offered to give him a bottle of wine if he would comply with their wishes. At length, though with much apparent reluctance, he agreed, on the condition that the wine should be immediately produced, and that the individual consented to receive the communication privately.

The Mason added, "Friend, if you do not confess to the company that I have shown you a Freemason's sign, I will pay for the wine myself." The proposition was too reasonable to be refused, and the curious candidate for Masonic knowledge retired into another room with his friend. Once there the Mason asked, "So friend, you are curious to see a Freemason's sign and can you keep a secret?"

"Try me," said his friend.

"Good! You know that our friend Johnson, the pub landlord, is a Mason?"

"Yes, I do," he replied.

"Very well." Then taking him by the arm, the Mason led him to the window. "Do you see the painting of the lion hanging from the bracket on the wall?"

"Of course I do – it's our landlord's sign."

"Good!" replied the Mason. "Then friend, since our landlord is a Freemason, are you satisfied that I have shown you a Freemason's sign, and that the bottle of wine is forfeited? For your own sake, you will keep the secret."

The man returned to the room with a look of astonishment and confessed that he had received the desired information. He then turned to another of the cowans, whispering,

"Do you want to see a sign of a Freemason? I'll show you for a bottle of wine."

•

A certain right Worshipful Sir was speeding down the road when he looked in his rear view mirror and saw the dreadful flashing lights. As he drove on he realised the policeman wanted to stop him, so he pulled over to the hard shoulder of the highway. The young policeman walked up to the driver's door and the R.W. Sir realised that to compound matters not only was he speeding, he was not wearing his seat belt. Whooommmp! On went the seat belt. The policeman knocked on the window and the R.W. Sir lowered the window.

The Officer said "Good evening R.W. Sir. Late for a Masonic meeting?"

The R.W. Sir thought to himself, 'this young man knows me, I don't know him, but I may get out of this ticket.'

"Ah, mmm! Yes, I am quite late. I should have been there 15 minutes ago."

The young policeman said, "R.W. Sir, I clocked you at 75 mph in a 55 mph limit, but I am willing to forgo the ticket if you can answer but one question for me." The R.W. Sir thought to himself, I have been Chairman of Education for a number of years. I should be able to answer any question this young man has. "Go ahead, ask me anything."

The policeman said, "Tell me R.W. Sir, do you find it difficult to steer the car with your seat belt through the steering wheel?"

●

A freemason parks his brand new Porsche in front of the Lodge to show it off to his Brethren.

The Sign of a Mason

As he gets out of the car, a lorry races along too close to the kerb and takes off the door before speeding off.

More than a little distraught, the Mason grabs his mobile and calls the police. Five minutes later, the police arrive. He starts screaming hysterically, "My Porsche, my beautiful red Porsche is ruined. No matter how long it takes at the panel beaters, it'll simply never be the same again!"

After the Brother finally finishes his rant, the policeman shakes his head in disgust: "I can't believe how materialistic you bloody Masons are. You lot are so focused on your possessions that you don't notice anything else in your life."

"How can you say such a thing at a time like this?" snaps the Brother.

The policeman replies, "Didn't you realise that your right arm was torn off when the lorry hit you?"

The Brother looks down in absolute horror, "Bloody Hell!" he screams. "Where's my Rolex?"

•

A very eminent Brother was driving along a busy street in London when ahead of him, a traffic light changed to red. The car in front stopped at the line and he dutifully took his place in the queue.

The lights changed to green and expecting to pull away any second, our V.W. Brother slipped the car into gear and hung on the handbrake. From the car in front? Nothing, it didn't even move an inch.

Being a patient soul, the V.W.B. waited and waited and eventually the lights returned to red. Not wishing to be stuck at the lights a moment longer, the second the lights went to green again, the V.W.B. leant on the horn when he was affronted by an arm out of the window in front with a middle finger stabbing the air.

He thought to himself 'I'm not putting up with that kind of rudeness, I'll have a word with the bastard.' He opened

the door, got out and strode towards the car in front.
On drawing level with the car, he looked in, saw a
little blue book on the seat next to the driver and said,
'I acknowledge the correctness of the sign!'

•

Q: How many Masons does it take to change a light bulb?
A: Two. One to search for the light and one to raise him
up.

•

MASONIC CRITICISM: We know that in the character
of a Master Mason, you are authorised to correct the errors
and irregularities of your uninformed Brethren and to
guard them against a breach of fidelity. But before
criticising a Brother, take heed of that old adage and never
criticise another until you have walked a mile in his shoes.
There are two good reasons for this. Firstly if he gets mad
at your criticism, you'll be a mile away. And secondly,
you've got his shoes.

●

SICKNESS AND DISTRESS:
When the Master asked about cases of sickness and
distress, it was reported that the Brother who had fallen
into the upholstery machine was now completely recovered.

●

BROTHERLY ADVICE:
"My Brother," said the old Past Master to the newly raised
Master Mason, "There are two secrets to success in life:
Number 1. Never tell people everything you know…"

●

MASONIC FUNERAL SERVICES:
In every Lodge or District there is always one faithful
Brother who officiates at most of the Masonic funeral
services. This story may be modified to fit him.

The local Funeral Director phoned the old Brother who
always performed the Masonic funeral services and said he
needed his help. It seemed that a body had been shipped
in from out of state with the instructions that a Masonic
graveside service be performed, and nothing more. The
departed Brother had no family or friends in the area, and
was to be buried in a small graveyard far out in the country
that very day. The faithful Brother said he would be glad to
provide a Masonic service for this Brother, so he put on his
black suit, stuck a sprig of evergreen in his breast pocket,
and headed out to the cemetery. He had never been there
before, and the instructions provided by the Funeral
Director were not too clear, and he soon found himself lost.
After driving up and down miles and miles of dirt roads,
he finally arrived about 45 minutes late. By that time, the
hearse was nowhere in sight and the vault was closed.
The workmen were leaning up against the backhoe, in the
shade of a tree, eating their lunch. Faithful to his trust,
the old Brother advanced to the head of the grave, alone,
and proceeded to deliver one of the best graveside services
that he had ever done. As he was making his way back to

his car, feeling happy about what he had been able to do, one of the workmen said to another, "Well, I ain't never seen anything like that before, and I've been puttin' in these septic tanks for 20 years."

●

A new Mason was constantly reviewing his E.A. work in preparation for his examination. He gave no thought to reciting this in front of his five year old daughter. One day while in the bathroom he heard a knock on the door and he immediately asked, "Who comes here?" The five year old responded, "A poor blind candidate and I need to pee."

●

A Mason was at work for the Post Office during the Christmas season. He noticed a letter addressed to Santa Claus. After a few minutes of study, he thought it wouldn't be against the rules to open a letter to Santa. The letter was from a woman who said she was a single mother and would he please send her £500 to buy presents for her children. The postman carried the letter to Lodge with him and they collected £400 which they appointed a committee to deliver in time for the mother to buy her children the presents. A few days later the postman again noticed a letter addressed to Santa and it was from the same address as the single mother. He promptly opened the letter which said, "Santa I really appreciate the money you sent me for my children, but next time please send it by someone else. The Masons kept £100 of it."

•

Two drunken Glaswegians staggered out of a pub in search of additional pintage when one got the idea to investigate the local Masonic lodge. "They've always got extra bevy in they places!" the first one said.

"But dae ye not haftae know wan o' they secret handshakes?" asked the second.

"You leave that tae me, pal! Nae bother!" replied the first, confidently.
The first old Scotsman strode up the hill towards the Lodge, only to come tumbling back down a few minutes later, clutching his face in obvious pain.

"What the devil happened, Jock? Could ye no' get us in?" asked the friend.

" I don't know what happened, Angus! There was a big strappin' laddie outside the front door. He asked me if I was a Mason, and I said yes. Then he said "Bo", and I said "Peep", and the bugger broke my nose!"

●

Brother Jones was just installed as the Worshipful Master of his Lodge. It was a cold night as he walked the four blocks to his home on that special night. He kept thinking of how his Brothers had paid so much respect to him on his elevation to that high office. It was his proudest moment as a Mason and he was now an installed leader of the craft!

His wife had already gone to bed, so he was careful not to wake her as he slowly slid under the warm blankets. As careful as he was, his foot touched his wife's leg, waking her. She shouted "God, your feet are cold!" He responded, "Sorry sweetheart, but you can still call me honey."

•

My favourite masonic joke is about the Entered Apprentice who knew too much. When he was asked why the North was a place of darkness, he answered that it's because that's where the Past Masters take their naps.

•

Q: How many Masons does it take to change a light bulb?
A: None. A Mason doesn't change a light. Masonic Light changes the man.

•

It was an exciting day for Freemasonry in Dublin. One of the Past Masters of the Lodge was appearing on the television quiz show Mastermind. His specialist subject: Freemasonry and its history. The questions started:

When was the Bail Bridge Square discovered?

"Pass."

When was the first Grand Lodge founded?

"Pass."

Who was the first Irish Grand Master?

"Pass."

Then a voice from the crowd piped up, "That's right, Paddy, don't you tell him nothing!"

●

Shortly before Christmas, three elderly Brethren were called to the Grand Lodge Above. On arrival at the Pearly Gates they were met by the Tyler (St. Peter). They were greeted well, but informed that due to a considerable amount of crowding at this time of year they would have to produce from about their person an item connected with Christmas to gain admission.

The first Brother felt in his pockets and produced a cigarette lighter. "What has that got to do with Christmas?" asked St. Peter. The Brother flicked the lighter into life and declared it was like a Christmas candle. "You may enter Brother."

The second Brother produced a bunch of keys. "And what relevance does that have to Christmas?" asked St. Peter. The Brother shook the keys and said they were like Jingle Bells. He too was granted admission.

The third Brother then delved deep into his pockets and finally, with some embarrassment, produced a pair of very frilly knickers. Not surprisingly St. Peter was somewhat astonished by this item and said, "What in Heaven's name has that got to do with Christmas?" The Brother, looking somewhat sheepishly replied, "They're Carol's!"

●

The funniest thing happened when we were getting a very nervous Army Officer ready to go into the Lodge. We asked him to salute the W.M as a Mason. Then next thing we knew he stamped his foot and gave a very smart military salute, with his hand quivering at his forehead.

●

Two young master Masons were driving home from an Installation Meeting at a Lodge some 200 miles from where they lived. Around midnight, in the middle of a snow storm, they decided it was too dangerous to drive any further. So they pulled into a nearby farm and asked the attractive lady who answered the door if they could spend the night.

"I realise the weather's terrible out there and I have this huge house all to myself, but I'm recently widowed," she explained. "I'm afraid the neighbours will talk if I let you stay in my house."

"Don't worry," Jack said. "We'll be happy to sleep in the barn. And as soon as the weather improves we'll be gone." The lady agreed, and the two Masons found their way to the barn and settled in for the night. Come morning, the weather had cleared and they got on their way and, as neither of them were married, there were no problems or explanations required when they got home.

About nine months later, Jack got an unexpected letter from a solicitor. It took him a few minutes to figure it out, but he finally determined that it was from the widow's solicitor.

He dropped in on his friend Bob and asked, "Bob, do you remember that good-looking widow from the farm we stayed at when we were caught in the snow about nine months ago?"

"Yes, I do," said Bob.

"Did you, er, happen to get up in the middle of the night, go up to the house and pay her a visit?"

"Well, um, yes," Bob said, a little embarrassed about being found out, "I have to admit that I did."

"And did you happen to give her my name instead of telling her yours?"

Bob's face turned bright red and he said, "Yeah, look I'm sorry, mate. I'm afraid I did. Why do you ask?"

"She's just died and left me everything."

●

The festive board is not only enjoyable for the food, but also for the humour that is so often a feature of the toasts one hears on those occasions. On one such instance when an English Brother was a visitor to a Barbados Lodge a native Barbadian Brother was nominated to propose a toast to him. He began by saying that when Barbadians are born, they are born black; when out in the sun, they remain black; and when they die, they die black!

But when an Englishman is born, he is born pink; when he is frightened, he turns white; when he is hot, he goes red; when he is cold, he goes blue; when he is ill, he turns green; when he is jaundiced, he goes yellow; when out in the sun, he goes brown; when enraged, he goes purple; and when he dies, he goes grey. So the one thing the Brother said he could never understand about the English is why they call the Barbadians coloured!

●

LONDON (EAST) RITUAL - OPENING THE LODGE

WM	OK Bruvvers, ere's the brief.
WM	Tickle them ivories John.
WM	Bruvvers, 'elp us to open this 'ere gaff
WM	Bruvver..... why do we 'ave to look lively?
JW	To make sure the wood's in the 'ole, Guvnor.
WM	Well, don't just stand there
JW to IG	OK, Bruvver.... you 'eard the Guv.
IG to JW	Done, John.
JW to WM	Done, Guv.
WM to SW	The next bit?
SW	To see that the Bruvvers are all in the firm.
WM	Come on, Bruvvers, shake a leg.
WM to JW	'ow much top brass in this 'ere drum?
JW	Free Guv. You and the two oppo's wiv the cuffs.
WM to SW	Bruvver SW, 'ow many others?
SW	Free John, besides the bouncer, namely the bloke on the door and the two geezers wiv the pool cues.

WM to JW	Where's the bouncer then?
JW	Outside the gaff, all tooled up.
WM	Why's that then?
JW	E's packing a blade in case we're busted Guv.
WM to SW	The bloke on the door?
SW	'overin abaht a bit.
WM	Wot the 'ell for?
SW	To check the tickets, admit new punters and do wot e's told by my oppo.
WM to JW	Where's the JD?
JW	Over there.
WM	Why?
JW	To grass to you, Guv and chivvy 'em all up a bit.
WM to SW	And the other one?
SW	Next to you Guv.
WM	Why?
SW	Errand boy, Guvnor.
WM to JW	Bruvver JW, wot abaht you?
JW	On the sidelines Guv.
WM	Why?

JW	To nip dahn the pub wiv the bruvvers, get some booze and grub, and get em all back 'ere before the last bell.
WM to SW	Bruvver SW, wot abaht you?
SW	Down the shallow end Guv.
WM	Wot the 'ell for?
SW	To let 'em know when its ligh'ing up time and to close down the gaff when all the bruvvers 'ave 'ad their cut.
WM to IPM	Where am I?
IPM	At the sharp end, Guv.
WM	Why's that then?
IPM	To keep them lot on their toes, open the gaff and get 'em at it.
WM	Bruvvers, now that we're all 'ere, its eyes down for a full 'ouse, but before we do, let's get the boss in the technical drawing department to tip us the wink so there's no aggro.
ALL	Nice one, Guvnor!